The Love Poems
of
Daniel Nanavati

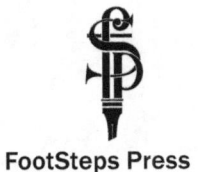

FootSteps Press

The love Poems of Daniel Nanavati
Published in the United Kingdom.
Footsteps Press First Edition

Typeset by Jenna Pascoe

ISBN 978-0-9566349-5-5

The Love Poems
of
Daniel Nanavati

Artwork by

Jonathon Xavier Coudrille

To The Woman I Loved

When The World Was

Twenty One

Poems

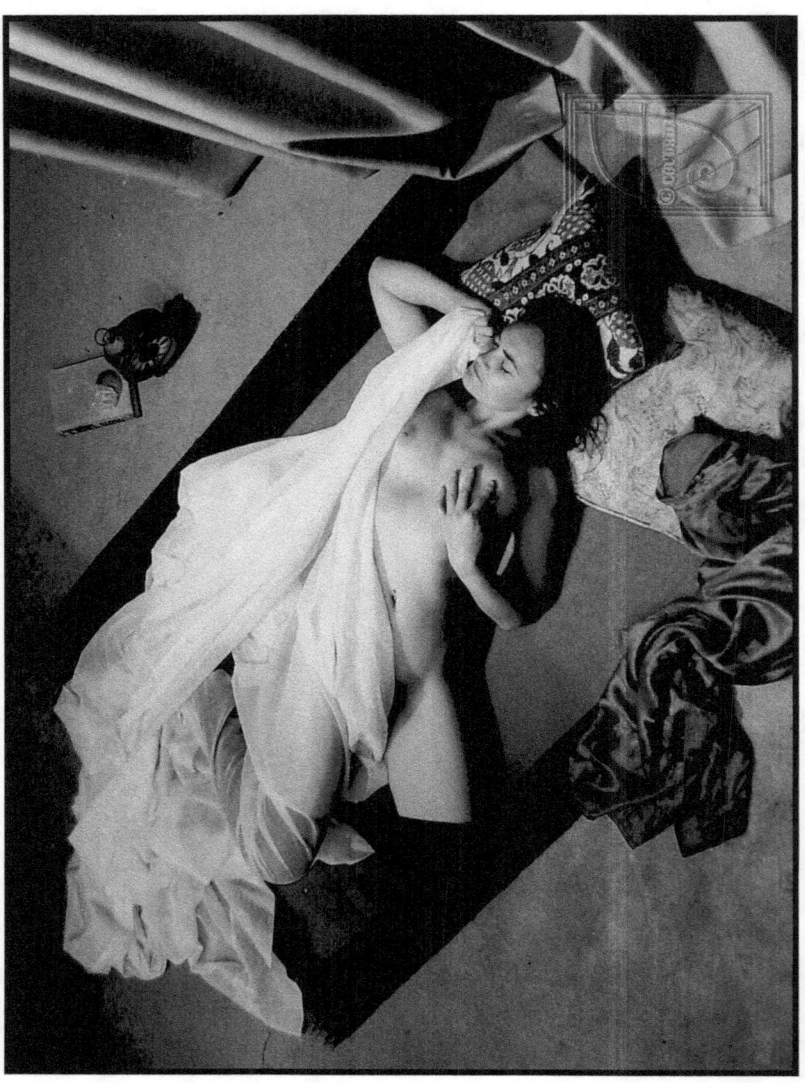

To Andrea

Life is not kind, her charity is to
Take away all we love in increments
Of substantial unsubtle pain and strew
A blizzard of tears into regiments
Whose strategy is to prove we live in
The shallow grave of time, barely covered
By anything we touch; for we are kin
To the sun, and sunlight has discovered
Us and planted her flag of life upon
Our hearts and superheated our senses
Until words, laughter and tears become one
And wisdom knows feelings have no fences.

Feelings are the sun within and their light
Is the personification of sight.

For J.B

There is an ambience in my lover's
Room which even in this stillness feeds my
Imagination, seeds the bed covers
With anticipated motion and lies
The floor with nakedness, enticing sounds
Only our ears hear to reverberate
Around the walls, till energy abounds
And two bodies moist and insatiate
Taste the air, feed on eyelid closeness, cap
The rhythm of the turning earth and turn
In time around the sun like an hour wrapped
In living, which is able to affirm

That souls may kiss and minds like limbs entwine
And time decant like any other wine.

For C.K

So much of nature loves and loves so much
May I love you? As the moon moves the sea
Timing tides and seasons without a touch;
As the sun sweeps the earth with the deep, free
Warmth of life; as the clouds bless the breeze to
Give it purpose and seeds seek the rain which
Moistens their growth to flowerhood. If you
Allowed I'd love you with a love as rich.
I'd be another moon, sun, clouds and seed
To your sea, earth, breeze and rain and we would
Love and from our love, a world we would feed
With happiness, if you but said we could.

The world's turning, like a ballet dancer
Caught in her flight, waiting for your answer.

Life

At the dawn of the cosmos chemicals
Precipitated – and all that was to
Be me was there. Hydrogen radicals,
Solidifying gases and a few
Trace metals bringing on the dawn of the
Earth and the colours of the rainbow which
My two brown eyes were created to see
And the wind with her harmonious pitch
Which my two ears were created to hear.
At the dawn of everything living, part
Of me knew, and everything is so near
Me now because I was there, at the start.

At every dawn to come, there I will be;
Only, for this while, is the dawn in me.

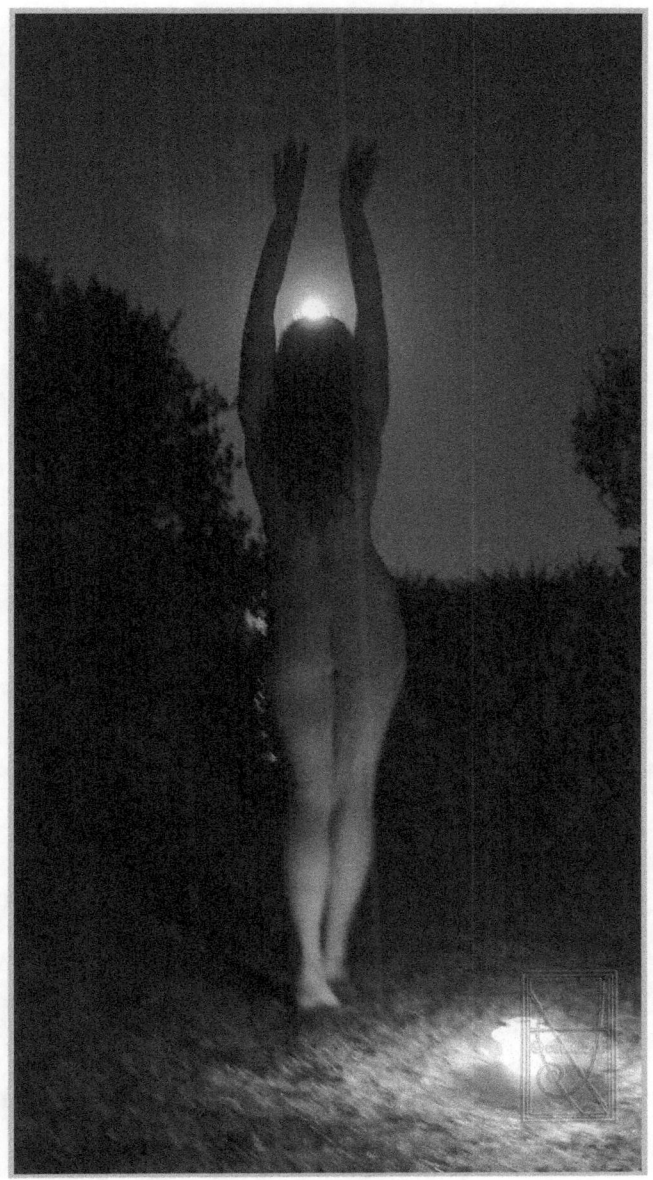

For C.K

The autumnal storms of time strip ideas

From my imagination like leaves from

A tree, which I shed on paper as tears

Of ink for roaming eyes to walk upon,

And in the rustling of thoughts grasp a vein

Of nature, which has waited for my pen

Language, books, paper before it attained

All that's necessary to be fallen.

If there were a new season in the year

It would come after autumn's collections

Of ideas and before winter's ice-clear

Winds and with it would come new emotions.

You are the newest season in my year

That grows within the leaf all I revere

Abelard and Helöise

Abelard loved the root in the plants, the
Wingedness of the birds, the power in
The oceans, the name of Helöise, the
Confluence of the natural world within
A woman's mind and form; where she breathes sense
Her voice like fruit-trees heavy with knowledge
Her soft skin translucent with recompense
Her eyes a spiritual patronage –
Abelard loved and was so loved Heaven
Would be incomplete without the other –
Helöise adored Abelard even
From torture cells where they could uncover

The rack of love, the fire of devotion
At one with the wild Atlantic Ocean.

The Cosmos

In all of cosmic time these hours resolve
Themselves upon me, testing my inner
Worth as their incessant seconds evolve,
Chasing me from my content to drier
Thoughts saturated by the light of stars
As old as dreams of heaven, and not the
Flood of gain behind the eyes popular
With the myth-makers of accountancy.
Once called by Time's infectious voice, I run
Across the space-less gulf which I control
And winged by dreams that I've alone begun
I meet my cosmos half way to my soul.

And how our laughter ricochets in space
As we dance away these hours, face-to-face.

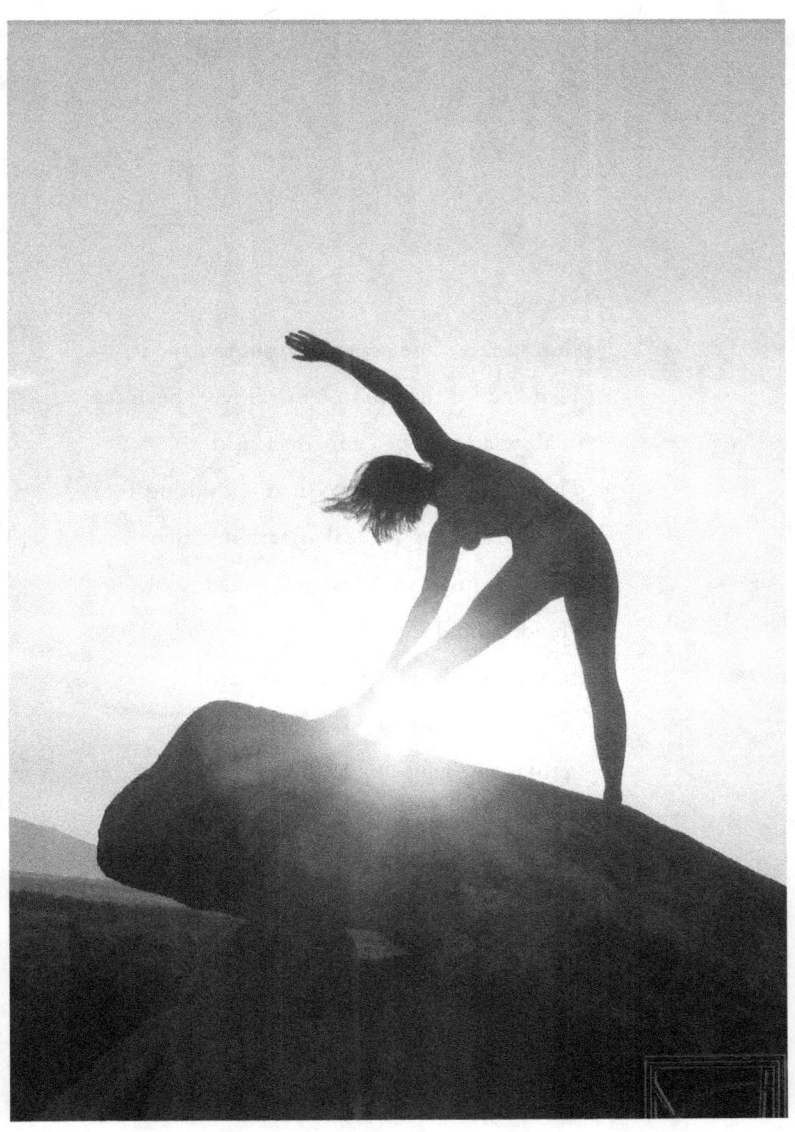

For G.A

I am scared to be borrowed and returned
Thanked for the use to which I have been put;
In all relationships I am concerned
That whorish transience shall not wrong-foot
The certain steps of real affection which
Walk the mind into sex - I so much wish
My ideals and thoughts to be at a pitch
Above anything that could be selfish.
And yet nothing in humanity is
Permanent, why should she be exempted?
Answering allure is a simple quiz,
A yes and yes is all that's expected.

I am weak enough to hunger and burn
Lust, not love, defines me at every turn.

For J.D

I chose June but the field marigolds chose
Me. I chose a primrose bank but open
Meadowlands chose you. We both chose the close
Of day but before a bird had spoken
Pre-dawn chose us. I wanted New England
And the soft luxury of the U.S
We found the shell beach at Trebarwith Strand
And all the inlets with which Cornwall's blessed.
Didn't you say you just wanted to dance
That your freedom was too precious to lose?
Didn't I promise this was just romance
Missing as I said it, all of the clues?

We chose to make love wherever the place –
All of the choices – put smiles on your face.

For J.W

What is the use of a bed without a
Woman upon it, to sculpture the sheets
With her form and the pillows with her play
And make the springs sing at her deep love's feats?
And what is the use of an hour of night
Or an hour of the day not resonant
With sighs and names? Darkness is far too light
And day too heavy when love's too distant.
And what is the use of waking before
Her if not to watch her face intently
Hoping, waking, it is you she looks for
Because you lie upon her mind, gently?

No dawn breaks as happy as those when she
Moves, opens her eyes, turns and looks for me.

To Andrea

Love is a word which proves that words have more
Than dictionary meaning because it
Is never intoned the same way twice nor
Isolated, but is a composite
Of persons, places, intents, feelings, thoughts
Beliefs, persuasions, attitudes and hopes.
The all important word that is self-taught
Buoyed in seas of language by which it floats.
It is a firework display of passions;
A warm blooded animal without veins,
Love is a hat that is out of fashion;
A motorway with far too many lanes.

When I run into your arms evolved dust
Alloys with sweat and kisses into us.

Art

If art is there to prove that people may
Attempt to prove they can create in time
A universe within the mind that sways
The heart as surely as the stars sway mine,
That makes the blood a river longing for
The sea, makes a microbe, stand for something,
Makes a tree a bone rooted to the core
Of every existence and every thing;
Then I have found that some Artists create
A greater world than money ever made –
For living for living's sake is a State
And loving because you can, is a trade.

Art's truly not a rarefied pursuit
But humanity's intimate tribute.

My Mother's Illness

You know, I do remember how it was
Picking primroses from hedgerows alive
With the rain whilst the sea breathed out salt because
That is its way of being perceptive.
The tenacious gorse gifted with perfume
Dancing candytuft and upright cowslips
And dogs, for whom Cornwall was their front room.
How the days had eyes and the night had lips.
Far away is youth in time and measure
Like an old experiment in some book
That wakens the mind to nature's treasure
Yet pulls at us, like some fisherman's hook.

Normality has flowed down to the beach
And filled some empty shells with empty speech.

Diane & Jan

Your eyes speak of my youth and my hand holds
Yours with that ease of emotion only
Years can grow; suppleness has changed to folds,
Wrinkles crease our nakedness, laughingly
The young would fun. What do they know? Your breasts
Suckled our children (and me once or twice),
And now our skins are thin, our love's contests
Are tactile drawings of our minds, which slice
Into our hours, sending ripples of sex
Around the day - I kissed your body in
To my being so now it is the text
From which I read - for everything - loving.

Tenderness does not age, how then can we?
Look into my eyes, see your youth in me!

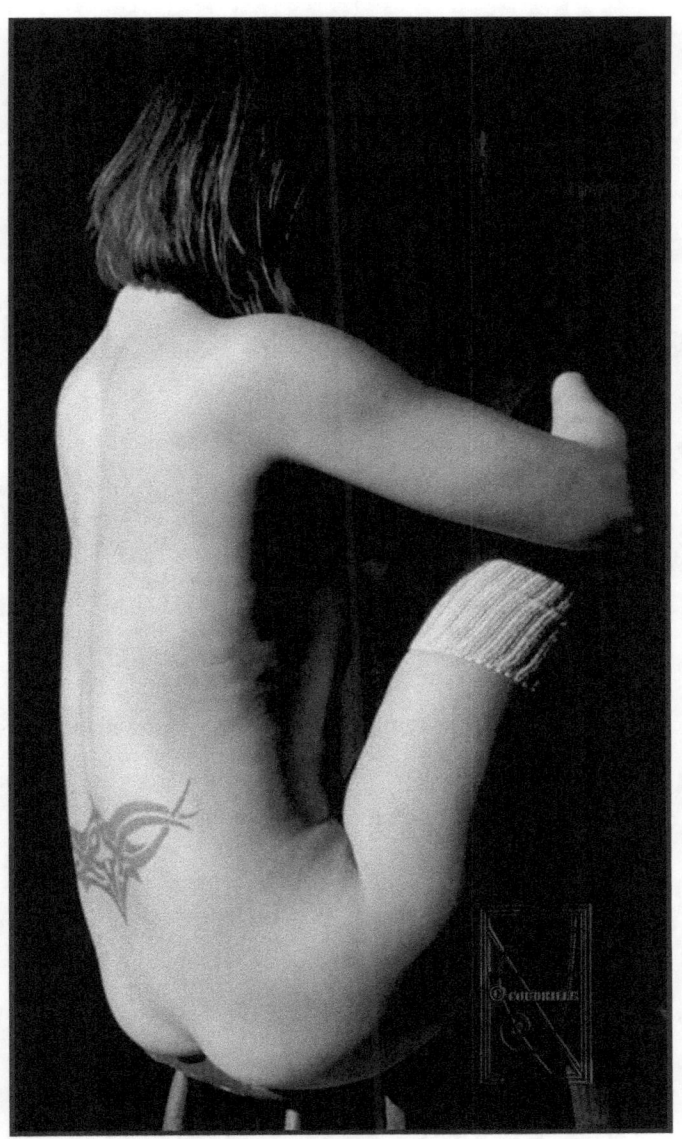

To Tammy

Do you love me with that respect which makes
Church certification irrelevant?
Where an unspoken understanding takes
Liquid time and from days makes a constant
Of shared experience? Can turn a tear to
Star light, a touch to passion and distance
To a longing to be at home with you?
I so much want to know if there's a chance
That that love is mine which warms you with a
Face, delights you with a voice, caresses
You every second; for which I would stay
Alive 'til the Universe undresses –

You've shown me your body loves me, be kind;
Show me you also love me with your mind.

Children

The glories of your heaven cannot show

A being quite as lovely to the eye

As one that through the days and months will grow

From babe to child, from child to mystery.

Inventions filter through your searching hands

Ideas shape and mold your every move

With grace you smile, with brilliance understand

What others took the centuries to prove.

The hours draw us closer to the time

When equals sit beneath a tiring sun

And from the chaos of the world confine

A million problems into only one.

Yet no matter how wise your words will be

In my heart you'll remain this child to me.

For B.C

I cannot hold the sun nor touch the moon
But I could hold your hand and touch your skin
And somewhere in a timeless afternoon
I could open my heart and let you in.
I cannot sway the sea or lower clouds
But with you by my side in your magic
Eyes I could make my kisses into crowds
And intimate words into a cosmic
Gallery of their own, filled with kitsch art
Of purple and blue, peopled with chics whose
Los Angelean faces are a part
Of American dreams and high heel shoes.

I will never own the stars, but much worse
If I lose you, I lose my universe.

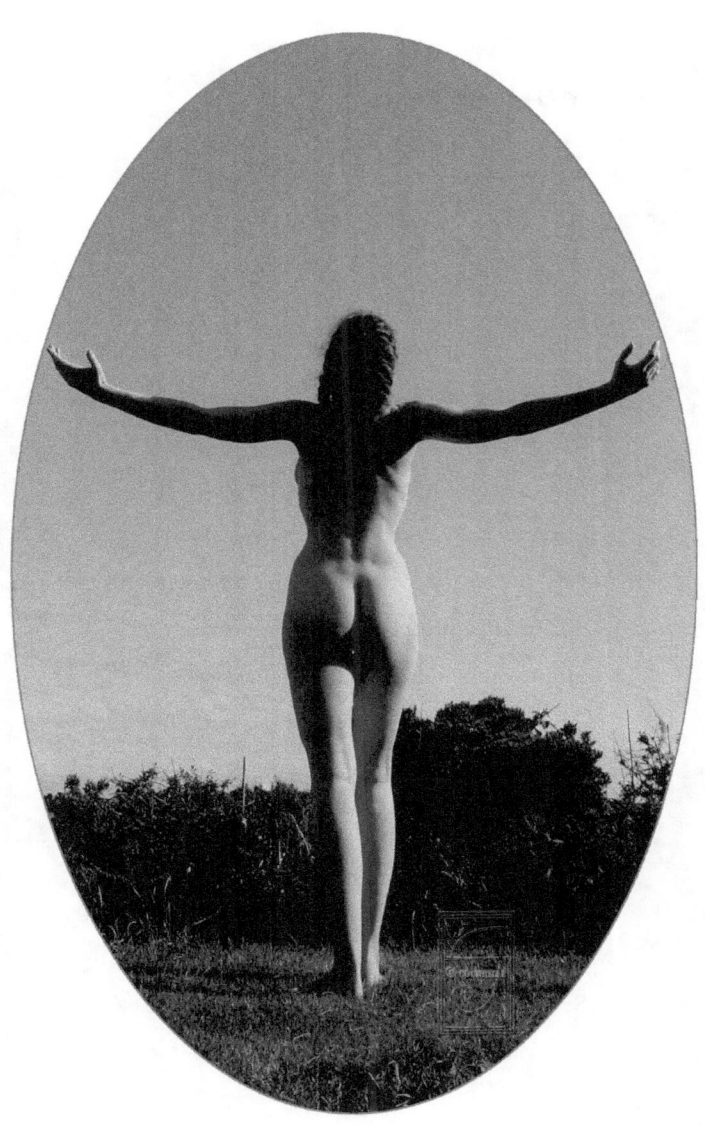

Marriage

The world does not know us as well as they
Think they do, only the sun and the stars
Can explain our love lighting up the way
For our souls like a painting on a vase
Circling the contents of the world each
Day and night; with footsteps which content me,
A climate atmospheric with your speech,
Hours on which I floated as if at sea.
The world simply doesn't know what I've lost
For it never wholly knew what we were
But I can tell the world, love has a cost
Which death extracts from all who embrace her.

You're no less my darling now, and that sun
Sparkles in words written for everyone.

To Tammy

I make love to the air when I accept
Her into me and the sea makes love to
Me when she lets me dive to test her depths
And my salted hand blows brief kisses through
The wavelets from salted lips to the stars
That created the world, which makes love with
Me each day as I learn love must be parsed
Like a sentence; her broken grammar gives
Me your name, a noun, and the coming for
You a verb and in the sub clause our lips,
Those adjectives like litter on the floor
Allow our designs and wishes to strip.

All nature moves in me as I move in
You like a bow across a violin.

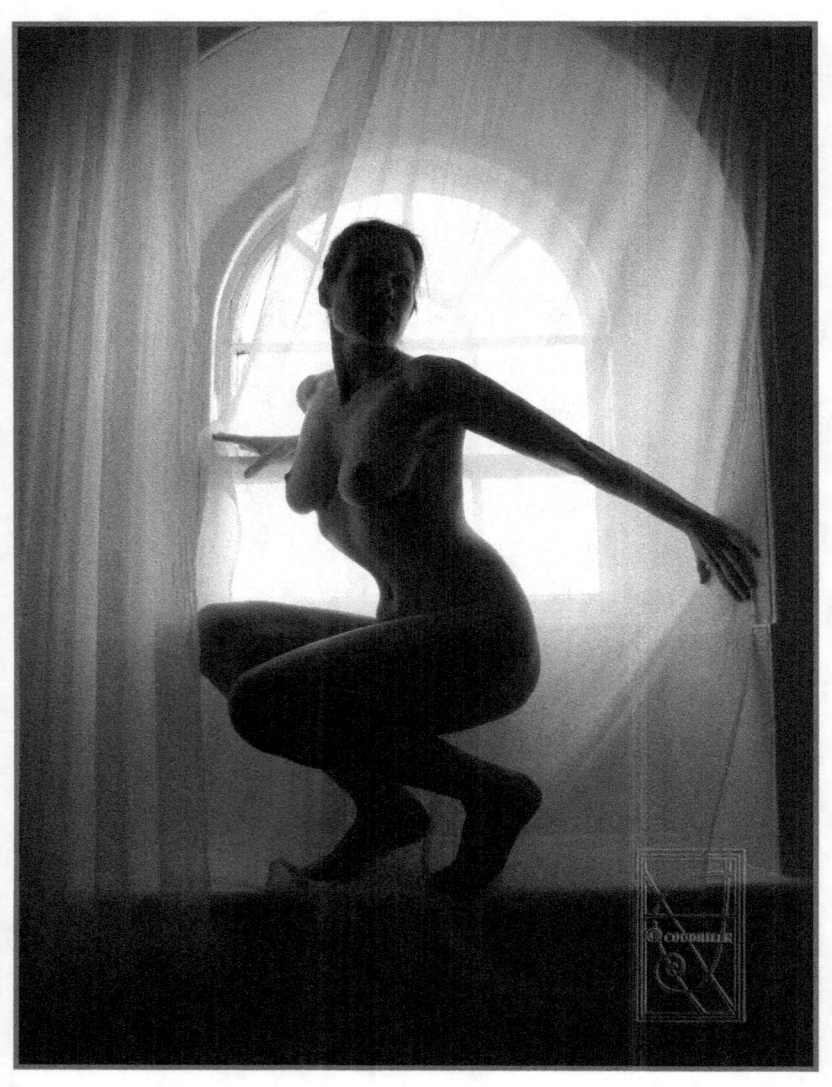

Love Remembered

Only when I am with you do I have
A sense of everything; of possession
And possessed, of the liberty in love,
Of the frank and easy conversation
Dovetailed with the intensity of your
Eyes and the waterfall of your ideas
Growing closeness like crystals in the pores
Of my skin, and the shadow which appears
And disappears with your departure and
Return; for your breathing is my heart beat
Your voice my blood flow, your desires my hands
Your caress my voice, your arms my retreat –

I have nothing left of myself but this,
In us I have everything self could wish.

Lost Love

I remember you, we loved once in the
Autumn, when we were to each other fruits
As delicious as any fresh cherry
Plucked in playful pairs as soft, round recruits
To an unplanned picnic. We had ripened
Where we had grown, watered by words to taste
Skin warmed by a sensuous sun, likened
I delight to recall, to perfumed lace.
Now I am here and you are here and years
Have passed and unwrinkled memory laughs
As the foggy distance between us clears
And reality splits itself in half.

And we nod, and we smile and we pass on
The crown of our Autumn forever gone.

Sex

Your body is a song to me, played to
The music of your sighs, as if passion
Were its own sun, shimmering within you
Directing my lips, as is their fashion,
With the balmy warmth of desire and touch,
As umouthed words coil around my tongue and
We begin to sing in harmony such
Songs as lovers sing, conducted by hands
That keep the heart-beat and the tempo in
The hour as our movements combine until
The long notes crescendo and with a twin
Ecstasy we gift to the other's will –

Sexual music illuminates the mind;
Yet, leaves us with everything else to find.

Goodbye

When the ship leaves the harbour or the plane
Leaves the runway and the baggage is packed
Before breakfast, or on the table train
Tickets laugh away the past and blood's sapped
From your feelings undermining any
Warmth, or the car's readied for the journey
You won't be taking and there are many
Mornings when you won't be able to see
Ahead of you – how do you say goodbye?
There are no clothes to wear, no fluid vow
No wisdom in an easy given lie
No softening of the cold here and now –

These pages are written into our lives;
Now let these pages be all that survives.

January

The atoms in the soil which grew this tree,
Might once have been a Brontosaurus' skin,
An early mammoth, horse, a chimpanzee,
Or men who dreamed of mining Cornish tin.
Some planets from a Universe must grow –
Whose life from stars is seeded in the seas;
For our existence is the ebb and flow
Of trees to people and people to trees.
One day I shall be part of a forest
With Bluebells and moss for my family
For the atoms within me cannot rest
As long as the earth lacks a single tree.

And though you will not recognise me quite
Still, wrap your arms around, and hold me tight.

From: The Beech Tree,1999

Passion

I touched your skin on the way to your heart;
I filled your eyes on the way to your mind;
The strength of desire I have made your Art;
The passion of knowledge, we have refined.
I touched your being and found my laughter
Then freed with your words, the being in me;
I touched a sense of forever-after
When I kissed you beneath the Galaxy.
The child you carry is far more than us
Beyond the depths of our humanity.
Beyond the passion and our Cosmic dust,
Beyond the touching dreams of sanity.

We touched, kissed and the stars evolved into
The rhythm of the river that is you.

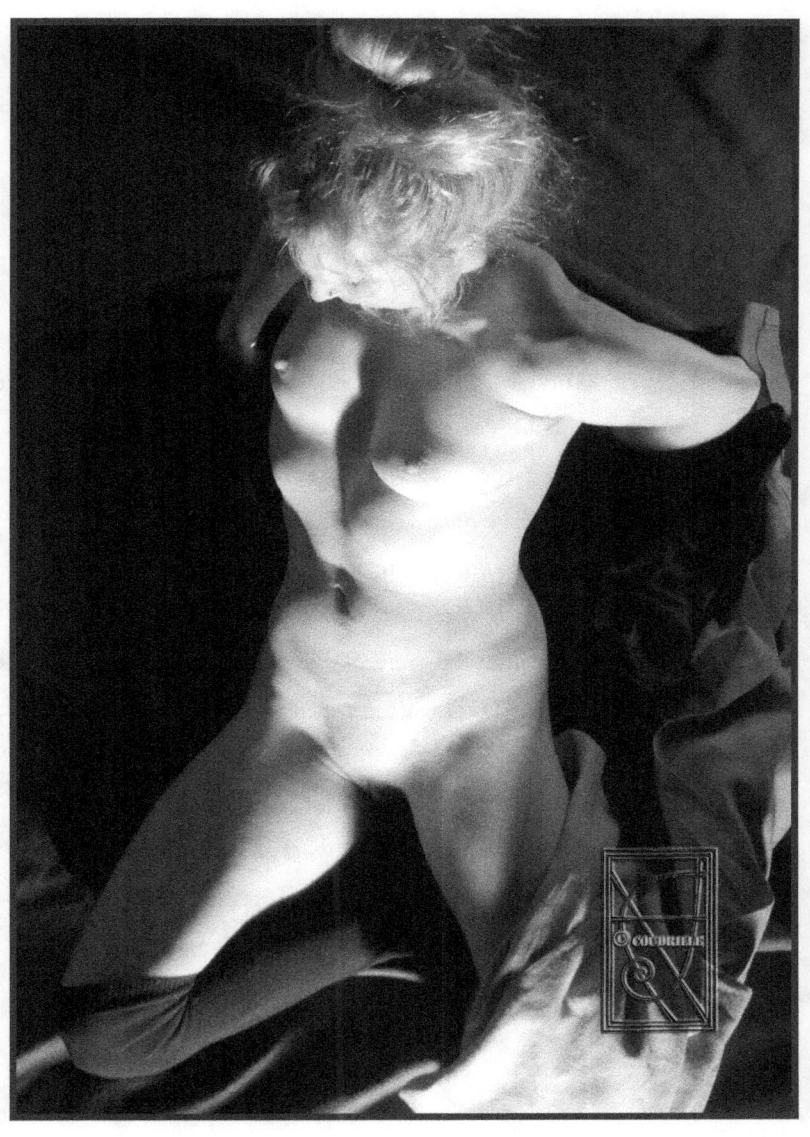

Future Readers

I lived – air on tongue, light on hair, skin sea
Touched, fingers horse maned, tired eyes soft-pillowed
A last loving, wall builder drinking tea
In a garden rich with roses, willowed.
My dirt hands wrote and dug, planted in ink
Seeded commas and sentences, infant
Words grown from experiences, thought-linked,
Stained in the grain of the woods, indifferent.
I lived. Saw the dead rotting from war waste
Hawked hatred sucking at lives like sweets
As if there were some glory in the taste
Mouth-rimmed like newborns at their mother's teats.

You live – and have seen what I've never seen
And taken my words where I've never been.

FootSteps Press Poetry

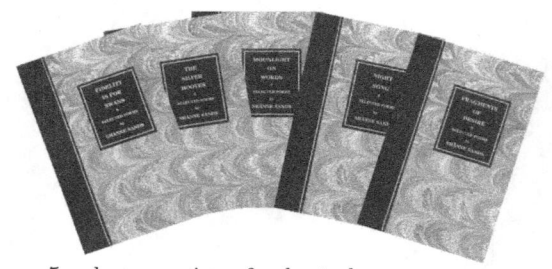

5 volume series of selected
poems by Shänne Sands:

Volume 1 :-   Fidelity is for Swans
Volume 2 :-   The Silver Hooves
Volume 3 :-   Moonlight on Words
Volume 4 :-   Night Song
Volume 5 :-   Fragments of Desire

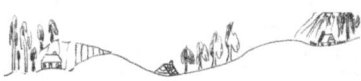

Incidental
illustrations
by the author

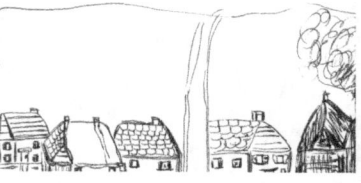

"One of the whole world's greatest poets."
Dr.Butler Brewton,
Furman University

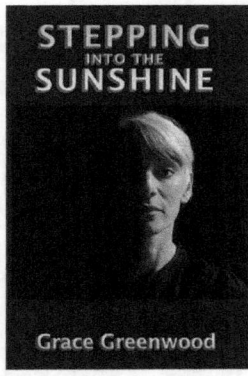

A poetry diary from Grace Greenwood capturing the essence of two successive abusive relationships. Why do women stay? Why don't they just leave?
How can someone reach rock bottom and turn their lives around?

In an honest portrayal of abuse, violence, love, betrayal, self-doubt and enormous courage, Grace lays bare some intense episodes in her life with a view to inspiring others, who find themselves in a very dark place to gather up the last bit of inner strength and join her by stepping into the sunshine themselves.

Paperback. 98 Pages.

ISBN 978-1-908867-00-1

"It should be on every person's 'must read' list."

Kimber Lee Cole

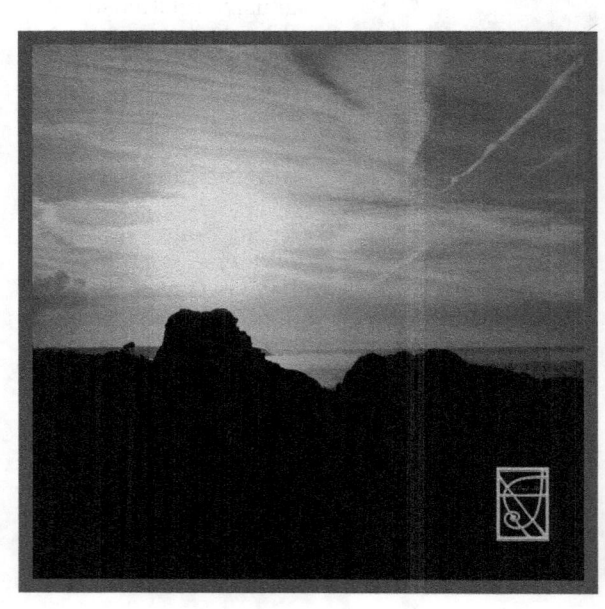

Images

www.ingramcontent.com/pod-product-compliance
Lightning Source LLC
Chambersburg PA
CBHW070433180526
45158CB00017B/1147